UNDERSTANDING

STARTUP

Double Your Chances for New Venture Success

UNDERSTANDING

STARTUP

Evidence-Based Entrepreneurship

CLINTON E. DAY

Alpharetta, GA

ISBN: 978-1-61005-777-6
Library of Congress Control Number: 2016906555

10 9 8 7 6 5 4 3 2 1 1 1 8 1 6

Printed in the United States of America

∞This paper meets the requirements of ANSI/NISO Z39.48-1992 (Permanence of Paper)

DEDICATION

To the next generation of game changers who will improve life, employ thousands, and help the underprivileged.

Willful waste brings woeful want.

~Thomas Fuller

Evidence-based lean or smart startup is the most important change to entrepreneurship education in fifty years. Yet most academic textbooks scarcely mention it, and entrepreneurs scramble to learn it. Hence, this anthology has been published to help everyone.

CONTENTS

Acknowledgments xiii

Introduction xv

General Philosophy 1

History of Evidence-Based Entrepreneurship 5

Core Methodology 9

Principles of Lean 13

Customer Development Method (CDM) 15

From Problem to Solution Using CDM 29

Use of the Business Model Canvas (BMC) 33

Agile Engineering 47

Disciplined Entrepreneurship 49

Value Capture—*The Lean Product Playbook* 53

Subtopics 57

- Comparison of Methodologies 57
- Concept of Pains and Gains 59
- Integration of a Business Plan 59
- New Venture Financing Cycle 60

Examples of Lean Startup Success 63

Where Evidence-Based Succeeds and Business Plans Fail 65

Other Important Model Discovery Books 69

The ULS* Course Map 81

- New Venture Discovery 83
- Interviewing End User 85
- Summary ULS Course Map 87

Glossary 89

Resources 101

Bibliography 103

About the Author 105

*ULS – Understanding Lean Startup

ACKNOWLEDGMENTS

Thanks to all who learned through experience and contributed to the design of evidence-based lean startup, particularly Steve Blank, Alexander Osterwalder, Eric Ries, Ash Mauyra, Taiichi Ohno, Dan Olsen, and Bill Aulet.

INTRODUCTION

Entrepreneurship as an academic discipline has been around forty-five years, gaining traction in colleges and universities during the 1990s. Until about 2008, business planning was based on a written business plan (summary, description, opportunity, marketing, financials, funding request, and appendices). Then, Silicon Valley produced a new and better way to plan new startups. Sometimes called lean or smart startup, evidence-based entrepreneurship is founded on business model discovery and uses a one-page tool, the business model canvas, created by Swiss consultants Osterwalder and Pigneur. The canvas allows entrepreneurs to search, find, and execute an idea for a product or service by using the feedback from targeted customers who confirm what they want. While outcomes depend on many factors and no single method can guarantee a favorable outcome, evidence-based entrepreneurship dramatically increases the chances for success.

After introduction of the *Entrepreneurship Quick Study Guide*, many entrepreneurs, accelerators, and students wanted to understand lean startup better as the preferred method to build a new venture. Most textbooks did not explain this alternative, evidence-based process. Instead, they spend time on traditional business planning rather than strong validation of the idea before spending precious time and money. This anthology brings together the many separate works on the topic, which together comprise lean or smart startup.

GENERAL PHILOSOPHY

Evidence-based entrepreneurship applies to new ventures launching under conditions of extreme uncertainty. The product, market, pricing, and fulfillment models are unknown and untested. Market responses to marketing action are unknown, so prior to validation a venture is unable to figure out the right business model. This method may not apply to startups where the model is already understood, such as in established franchises and familiar small businesses like a neighborhood dry cleaner.

Lean or smart startup entrepreneurship is a scientific approach to creating and managing startups. Simply stated, it is validated learning. The main reason products/services fail is because they don't meet customer needs in a way that is better than alternatives. If startups invest their time into building products or services "iteratively" to meet the needs of early customers, they can reduce the market risks and sidestep the need for large amounts of initial funding, and avoid product launch failures. The startup begins with a basic product known as the minimum viable product (MVP) that allows the startup to learn market responses with little investment in development.

Rapid iteration (repetition of a process) allows a team to discover a feasible path toward a "product/market fit." Lean startup enables entrepreneurs to efficiently build a startup by searching for the product/market fit rather than relying on costly research.

Evidence-based entrepreneurship has three components: one is business model design, two is customer development, and three is agile engineering. Together, these three components help startups become efficient, reducing the amount of time to get to the first product and the amount of cash necessary to build it.

Customer development (CD) is the formal process of testing hypotheses about the business model in a search for developing a match between customer problems and solutions. It is done almost entirely "outside the building" in front of customers, partners, and stakeholders. Business founders should be members and lead the team in the field.

CD involves collecting data and looking for insight into that data. It is a kind of entrepreneurial science. The MVP, minimum viable product, is the simplest thing you can show the customer to elicit a response. We call what we need to know about customers the "customer archetype." You are trying to live a day in the life of that customer and find out characteristics of their life. It helps to gain insight into your buyer's persona and expectations and to understand their journey.

The business model canvas (BMC) starts with the value proposition, which is where your company's product intersects with a customer's desire. It is the fit between an important problem that customers face and the solution you are providing to that problem. A value proposition canvas compares the jobs a product or service should do and the gains and pains the customer feels.

Scale and growth are not possible until the business model has been tested and validated. Once there is an established demand sometime during the end of the first and beginning of the second stage in the startup financial cycle, the new venture can then be funded, expanded, and sustained.

Agile development introduces the human factor by adding customer collaboration. It rose from software development, in which solutions grew from collaboration between self-organizing, cross-functional teams. Agile development promotes adaptive planning and continuous improvement.

The four "bibles" of lean startup are *Business Model Generation* by Osterwalder and Pigneur, *The Startup Owner's Manual* by Steve Blank and Bob Dorf, *The Entrepreneur's Guide to Customer Development* by Brant Cooper and Patrick Vlaskovits, and *The Lean Startup* written by Eric Ries.

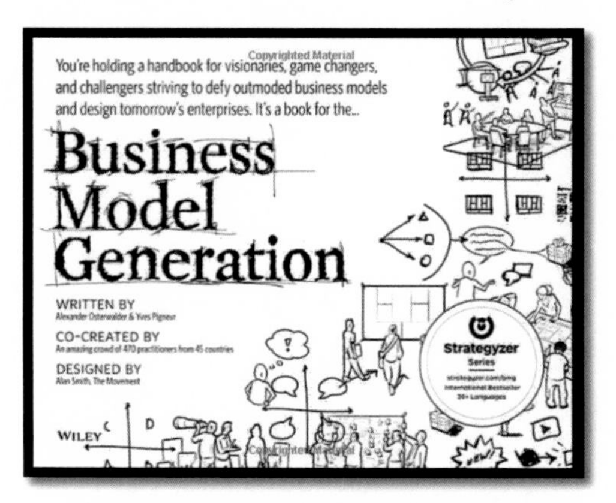

Alexander Osterwalder, *Business Model Generation* (Hoboken, New Jersey: John Wiley & Sons, 2010).

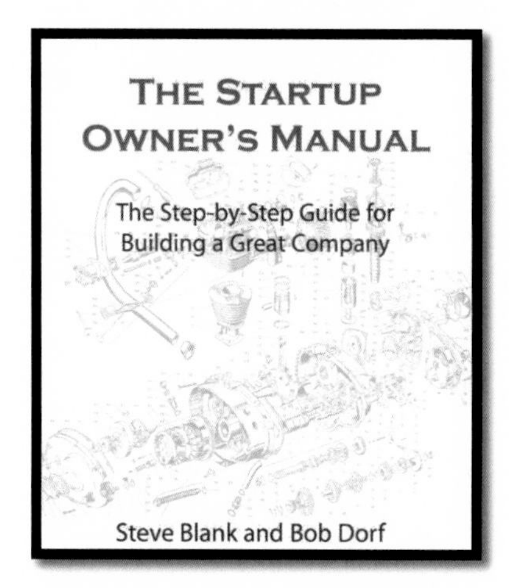

Steve Blank and Bob Dorf, *The Startup Owner's Manual* (Pescadero, California: K&S Ranch, Inc., 2012).

Brant Cooper and Patrick Vlaskovits, *The Entrepreneur's Guide to Customer Development* (Cooper-Vlaskovits, 2010).

Eric Ries, *The Lean Startup* (New York: Crown Business, 2011).

HISTORY OF EVIDENCE-BASED ENTREPRENEURSHIP

- The breakthrough came when traditional business plans did not work for tech startups
    - Startups are not smaller versions of established businesses
    - New tools were needed for unknown, innovative business models
    - Disjointed practices were integrated into a coherent method
- Traditional business plans failed in key areas
    - Static document that relied on secondary market research
    - No way to measure return on investment (ROI)
    - Financial projections, pro forma assumptions rejected by market
- Applied the scientific method to entrepreneurship
    - Observe, predict, experiment, and control adapted
    - Customer discovery using a hypothesis in the experiment
    - Discovery findings are key to the process
- Developed by Toyota, Steve Blank, Eric Ries, and Babson College

    - Based on lean manufacturing pioneered by Toyota's Taiichi Ohno
    - Production system included seven wastes and just-in-time concepts
    - Waste is anything other than the creation of value for an end customer
- Swiss Alexander Osterwalder invented the Business Model Canvas (BMC)
    - Firm's product is visually displayed using nine canvas building blocks
    - Right side is about value delivery, left side about "backbone" structure
    - Value proposition's relationship to customer is key (product/market fit)
- Steve Blank began the movement with *Four Steps to the Epiphany* (2003)
    - Idea of hypothesis can be validated using parts of a business model
    - Entrepreneurship can be actively managed vs. passively experienced
    - His customer development methodology cornerstone of lean startup
- Ash Maurya wrote *Running Lean* (2010), inspired by *Four Steps to the Epiphany*
    - Goals of creating an actionable guide for web-based entrepreneurs
    - Designed a new canvas (the Lean Canvas) from ideation to exit

    - Provides a systematic process for iterating from Plan A to success
- Eric Ries, a student in Blank's first customer development class at the University of California, Berkeley
    - Refined agile development and wrote *The Lean Startup* (2011)
    - Iterative products and hypothesis drive experimentation and save time
    - Customer feedback creates validated learning, the essence of lean startup

CORE METHODOLOGY

Feasibility determines the degree to which a product or service idea appeals to potential customers and identifies the resources necessary to produce it. The question is not "Will the idea work?" but rather, "Is there a market for the idea?" Entrepreneurs need a lot of feedback from potential customers to successfully answer the question, "Are customers willing to purchase our goods and services?"

The mistake in the past was reliance on primary and secondary research to reach conclusions. Too often incomplete information gave a false reading to proceed with a new business, overlooking data that would not have supported a market demand. Past surveys, questionnaires, focus groups, and "windshield" research were not enough. Instead, lean startup relies on a prototype or hypothesis in front of targeted customers, giving entrepreneurs opportunities to fix solutions to unforeseen problems.

Swiss consultants Osterwalder and Pigneur studied successful entrepreneurs, and then created a new method for startup analysis. They designed a business model composed of nine elements common to the successful startups and noticed most ideas began visually as a diagram. Their "canvas" shifted feasibility analysis from a business plan to construction of a business model, which describes the rationale of how an organization creates, delivers, and captures value.

During the feasibility analysis, this graphic process adds more detail to an evaluation. Entrepreneurs can compare the business's moving parts to see how they work together under each of the BMC components. The Osterwalder-Pigneur findings were used to develop a framework to guide the process of testing and refining the business model.

Ash Maurya, author of *Running Lean*, adapted the BMC to better track the evolution of the model's iterations and pivots into the "lean canvas" shown below. As a web designer, Maurya wanted more emphasis on problem/solution before product/market fit to simplify the hypotheses to a smaller set of questions—what, who, and how. What is the problem you are trying to solve, who has the problem, and how to solve the problem, reach the customer, drive demand, and make money?

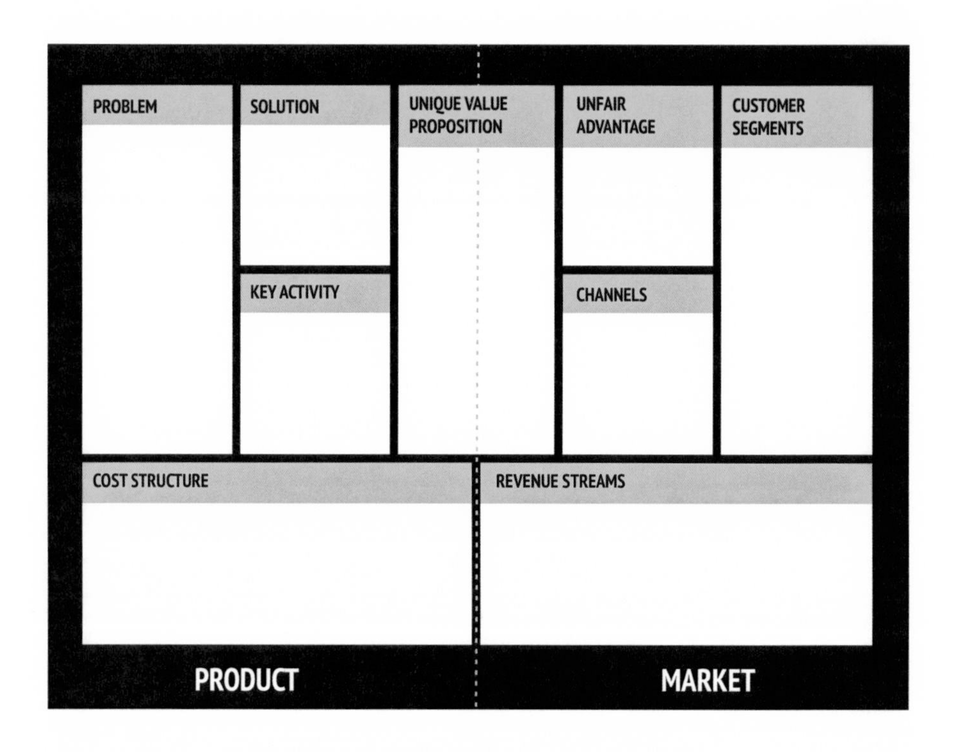

Adapted from *Running Lean*, Ash Maurya (2012).

ASH PROVIDES TEN STEPS TO PRODUCT/MARKET FIT:

1. Your product is not "product"
2. Explore different models and prioritize where to start
3. Understand three stages of startups:
   Problem/Solution Fit, Product/Market Fit, Scale
4. Focus on the right metrics
5. Formulate falsifiable hypotheses
6. Architect for learning
7. Architect for speed
8. Go only as fast as you can learn
9. Validate qualitatively, verify quantitatively
10. Systematically test your model

It is important to keep the "burn rate," the rate at which enterprise spends money in excess of income, as low as possible while iterating toward product/market fit. Hypotheses need to be turned into facts. The Lean LaunchPad course requires ten customer interactions between classes and as many as four hundred over the course. It can take countless interviews to gather enough customer information to render an idea valid.

PRINCIPLES OF LEAN

"Lean" emanates from Japan, where it was invented by Toyota and known as Muda or wastes under the Toyota Production System. Its principles were Value, Value Stream, Flow, Pull, and Perfection. Lean Japanese methods use less of everything—human effort, capital investment, facilities, inventories, and time. Its father was Taiichi Ohno, who came to Toyota in 1932 and rose to supervise the engine manufacturing process, during which he coined the Just In Time (JIT) and the Seven Wastes concepts.

SEVEN WASTES OF LEAN:

1. Delays, waiting, or time spent in a queue with no value being added
2. Producing more than you need
3. Over processing or undertaking non-value added activity
4. Transportation
5. Unnecessary movement or motion
6. Inventory
7. Reduction of defects

CUSTOMER DEVELOPMENT METHOD (CDM)

Steve Blank spent thirty-four years in high tech founding or working in eight startup companies, four of which went public. His eighth was customer relationship provider E.piphany, and, after retiring, he wrote *The Four Steps to the Epiphany*, a book that detailed his approach to the customer development process. His 2003 book explains how entrepreneurship is a practice that can be actively managed rather than an art, which must be passively experienced.

One of his first students at UC Berkeley, Eric Ries, added the notion of agile development and called the process "the Lean Startup." Together these two recognized that building a business is more than just creating a product and hoping people buy it. Entrepreneurs need to create and validate all aspects of their business model to make sure its pieces fit together. These two pioneers built on their original vision, with Steve designing the Lean LaunchPad course taught at major universities and Eric writing the best seller *The Lean Startup*. Ries designed the Build-Measure-Learn loop below to describe the agile development process:

Customer Development Method (CDM)

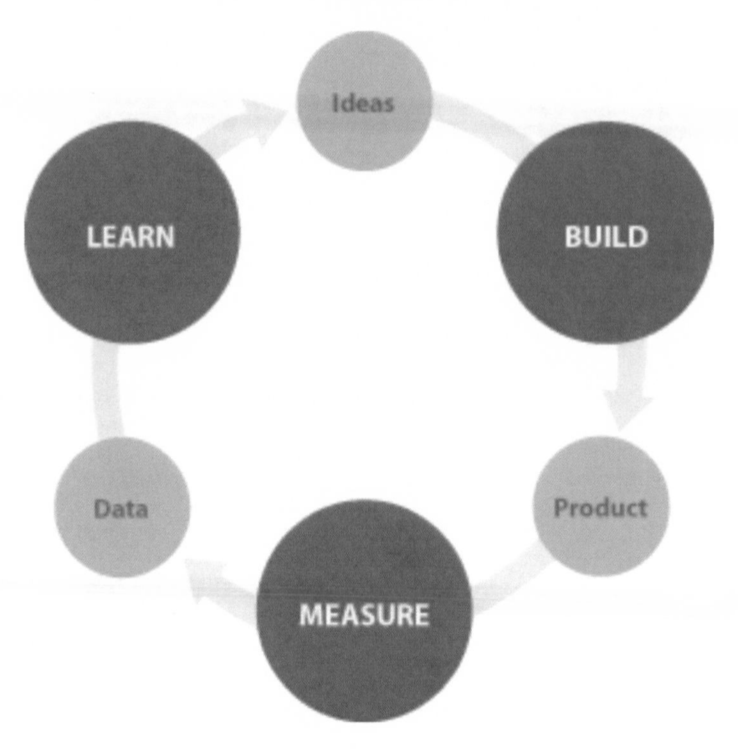

Adapted from *The Lean Startup*, Eric Ries (2011).

Steering Wheel Loop

Blank's Lean LaunchPad course uses the BMC as its primary design tool, whereas Eric's *The Lean Startup* fosters companies to be more capital efficient and uses a feedback loop to steer testing. Both rely on validated learning, rapid scientific experimentation, practices that shorten development cycles, measuring actual progress, and determining what customers really want. At UC Berkeley, mentors are paired with LaunchPad teams, and they along with faculty, experienced entrepreneurs, and venture capitalists act as instructors who guide students through their testing.

Steve pioneered much of the work that has combined the BMC and customer development. Together these elements fit together to produce a new idea into a successful business. Key steps under the BMC are:

1. **Customer segment analysis.** Knowing the profile, problems, and expected advantages of a potential customer helps form the product and its marketing strategy. An important part of the model is the initial value proposition and its product/market fit:

   a. The product/market fit is the relationship between the most important components of the BMC, the value proposition (the idea for a product or a service), and the customer segment (or the customer target market). The interaction between these two components gets the dialogue going to gather as much information as possible from the potential customer. *See Value Proposition Canvas in "Use of the Business Model Canvas" chapter.*

   b. Osterwalder's Strategyzer company produced a second book and second canvas called *Value Proposition Design*, which provides specifics on how to create value for customers by helping design products and services customers want. It identifies advantages customers gain by purchasing a particular product and better describes the hypotheses underlying the business model.

Product-Market Fit

The Product-Market Fit is the degree to which a product satisfies a strong market demand to allow the expenditure of capital to scale a company.

Value Proposition

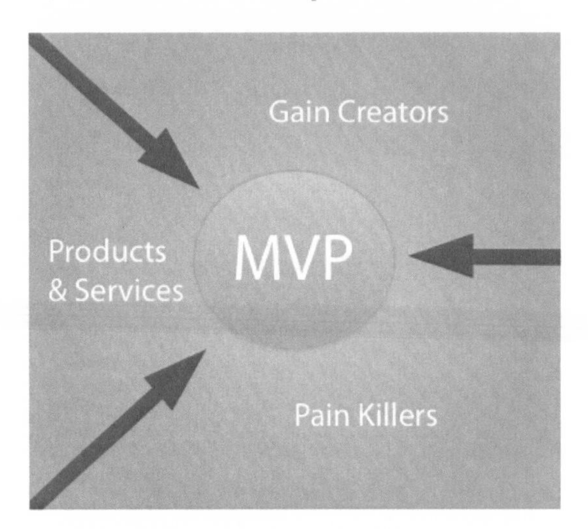

Customer Segment

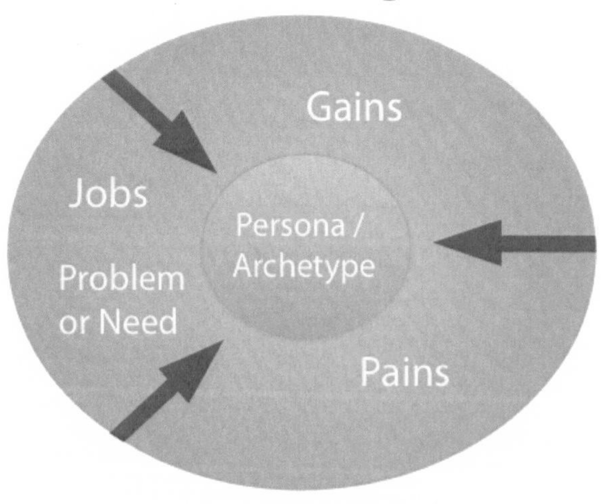

Adapted from *Value Proposition Design*, Alexander Osterwalder and Yves Pigneur (2014).

2. **Customer relationships.** Build customer relationships in both physical and digital channels to acquire, keep, and grow a customer base. Includes personal services in the form of employee-customer interaction, self-service, or indirect interaction between the company and the clients, automated services like Amazon recommendations based upon a purchase, creation of client communities, and co-creation, which is a personal relationship created by customers' direct input.

3. **Creation of a Minimum Viable Product (MVP).** This is the first iteration of the most basic features that allow you to charge customers for the product they want that improves as it moves through the customer development process. Its sole purpose is to run experiments to gain customer feedback, and the MVP has only core features that allow a product to be deployed and no more. The strategy behind it is to avoid building products that customers do not want and to maximize information about the customer's wants and needs.

4. **Revenue model.** This section helps shape a revenue model from different streams unique to each customer segment, information critical to the financial health of a startup. Earnings are figured by subtracting the costs from revenue generated from each customer segment. Startups must evaluate the worth of the value they provide to each customer segment. Details such as pricing and projected lifecycles make it possible to evaluate whether to use a revenue stream or not.

The Customer Development (CD) process developed by Steve Blank in *The Four Steps to the Epiphany* allows one to learn "by getting out of the building" and testing key ideas and features of their idea as quickly as possible using the framework of Osterwalder's BMC:

1. The BMC nine-box diagram lays out your hypotheses, customers, the product or service, its marketing channel(s), how it makes money, and what is needed as resource, and then new renditions of updated BMCs keep track of the testing and changes.

2. Interaction with potential customers involves showing them prototypes of the hypotheses such as clay models, diagrams, photos, and so forth to get the dialogue going and gather as much information as possible. If the hypotheses turn out to be wrong, we change them through pivots or a substantive change to one or more of the business model components. If the change is minor, we tweak parts of the BMC and call it an iteration.

3. Customer discovery means trying to answer questions about who the customer is, what the problem is, and what solutions might solve the problem. An entrepreneur asks these questions for each segment of the canvas, the customer, the partners, cost and revenue streams, and activities. The discovery involves designing the experiments, asking the questions, and recording the results.

4. Because only the founders or originators of the idea/hypothesis can make changes on the spot, it is important they are included in the team working outside the building in the field with target customers. They have the authority to gather the information and pivot or iterate immediately to keep the process going.

5. Entrepreneurs are not just collecting data, but looking for insights. Data is only as good as the "aha" or understanding it brings to the idea. Steve Blank, the godfather of customer discovery, likes to say, "We're not accountants here," and "accountants don't run startups." One is looking for what happens as the MVP evolves and becomes more valuable.

6. Knowing everything possible about the potential customers is called the "customer archetype." Potential customers are the ones who create demand, and you want to know where they are and what constitutes a day in the life of the customer. You're asking not only what do they do during the day, but what do they read, listen to, and buy? The goal is getting, keeping, and growing customers. The right side of the BMC everyone can see, but the left side operates more behind the scenes.

Business Model Canvas (BMC)— Questions Per Component

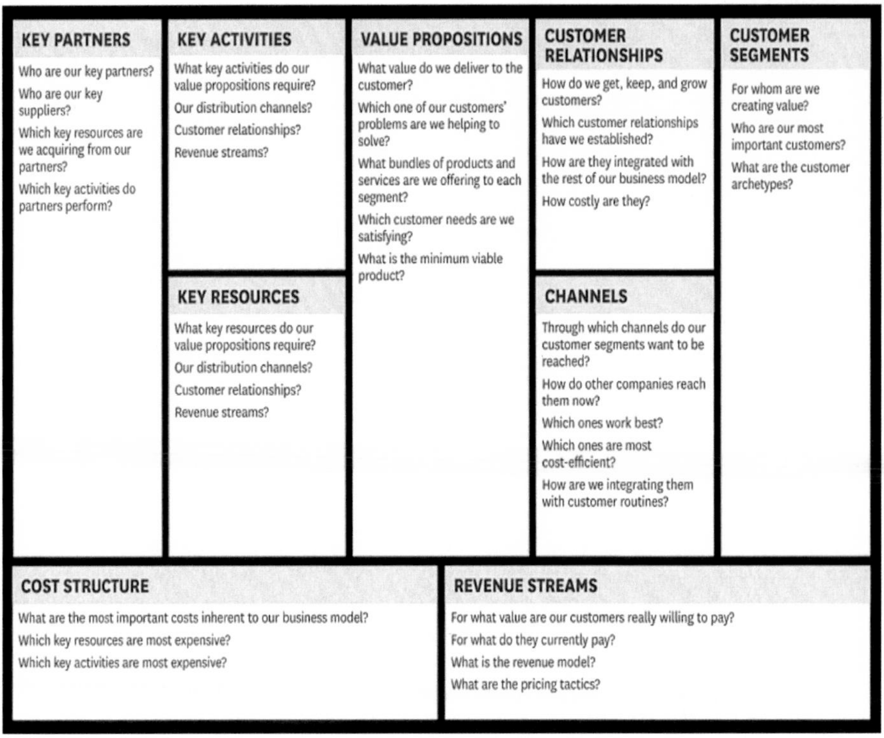

KEY PARTNERS
Who are our key partners?
Who are our key suppliers?
Which key resources are we acquiring from our partners?
Which key activities do partners perform?

KEY ACTIVITIES
What key activities do our value propositions require?
Our distribution channels?
Customer relationships?
Revenue streams?

KEY RESOURCES
What key resources do our value propositions require?
Our distribution channels?
Customer relationships?
Revenue streams?

VALUE PROPOSITIONS
What value do we deliver to the customer?
Which one of our customers' problems are we helping to solve?
What bundles of products and services are we offering to each segment?
Which customer needs are we satisfying?
What is the minimum viable product?

CUSTOMER RELATIONSHIPS
How do we get, keep, and grow customers?
Which customer relationships have we established?
How are they integrated with the rest of our business model?
How costly are they?

CHANNELS
Through which channels do our customer segments want to be reached?
How do other companies reach them now?
Which ones work best?
Which ones are most cost-efficient?
How are we integrating them with customer routines?

CUSTOMER SEGMENTS
For whom are we creating value?
Who are our most important customers?
What are the customer archetypes?

COST STRUCTURE
What are the most important costs inherent to our business model?
Which key resources are most expensive?
Which key activities are most expensive?

REVENUE STREAMS
For what value are our customers really willing to pay?
For what do they currently pay?
What is the revenue model?
What are the pricing tactics?

Adapted from *Business Model Generation*,
Alexander Osterwalder and Yves Pigneur (2010).

Blank is generous to share his work. On his website he provides past and present results from lean startup activities[1]. To quote why we need to understand customers, "We think we need to come up with some kind of prototype first, but first we need to select which customers we're going to address and we

[1] "Entrepreneurs are Everywhere," on Steve Blank's official website, published March 1, 2016, http://steveblank.com/2016/03/01/entrepreneurs-are-everywhere-show-no-23-nina-tandon-and-brandon-mcnaughton/.

need to deeply understand them. . . You don't want to work for just any kind of customers, but customers that have a budget, that are willing to buy from you. Because at the end of the day a business model only survives if it can be profitable."[2]

Subtitled "The Step-By-Step Guide to Building a Great Company," the *Startup Owner's Manual* is the bible for the customer development methodology. In one phrase, it is "to get out of the building" to search for a repeatable and profitable business model by questioning target markets. Products developed by founders who "get out of the building" early and often succeed because outside is where customers live and where entrepreneurs can transform their guesses into facts. It gives deeper understanding of customer needs and combines the knowledge with incremental and iterative product development.

Customer development involves validating the proper market for your idea, building the right product, testing the correct model, finding tactics to acquire customers, and building the best organization to scale the business. Rather than assume beliefs are true, customer development applies the scientific method to building a business through validation of products, procedures, and services. It helps a business become focused, capital and resource efficient, and is much more likely to find a product/market fit to gain traction in the market.

[2] "Explains the Business Model Canvas," by Steve Blank, Episode 1 on Sirius XM Ch. 111, July 4, 2015, http://steveblank.com/2015/07/14/episode-1-on-sirius-xm-channel-111-alexander-osterwalder-and-oren-jacob/.

THREE PHASES OF THE CUSTOMER DISCOVERY ARE:

1. Problem/solution fit (validate with prospects that problem exists)
2. Validate the solution using MVP that demonstrates the solution
3. A sales and marketing path (maps out the customer's buying process)

Until a hypothesis has been validated through the customer development process, any assumptions by entrepreneurs are nothing but guesses. Success comes from locating real customers, soliciting their feedback, and analyzing the problems to be solved.

Customer Segmentation

- What do you do professionally?
- Who handles [process you're improving] at your home/office?
- Tell me about your role at [company].
- How much time do you spend on [process you're improving]?

Problem Discovery

- What's the hardest part of your day?
- What are some unmet needs you have?
- What product do you wish you had that doesn't exist yet?

- What tasks take up the most time in your day?
- What could be done to improve your experience with [process/role]?
- What's the hardest part about being a [demographic]?
- What are your biggest/most important professional responsibilities/goals?

Problem Validation

- Do you find it hard to [process/problem]?
- How important is [value you're delivering] to you?
- Tell me about the last time you [process you're improving].
- How motivated are you to solve/improve [problem/process]?
- If you had a solution to this problem, what would it mean to you/how would it affect you?

Product Discovery

- What would your ideal solution to this problem look like?
- What's the hardest part about [process you're improving]?
- What are you currently doing to solve this problem/get this value?
- What do you like and dislike about [competing product or solution]?

Product Validation

- Would this product solve your problem?
- How likely are you/would you be to tell your friends about this product?
- Would you ever use this product?
- What might prevent you from using this product?
- Will you pay [dollar amount] for this product?

Product Optimization

- What could be done to improve this product?
- What would make you want to tell your friends about this product?
- What's most appealing to you about this product?
- What motivates you to continue using this product?
- What's the hardest part about using this product?
- What features do you wish the product had?

Ending Interviews

- [Summarize some of your key takeaways] Is that accurate?
- So based on the conversation, it sounds like x is really hard for you, but y is not. How accurate is that?
- It sounds like x is very important to you, while y is not. How accurate is that?
- Is there anything else you think I should know about that I didn't ask?

- Do you know anyone else who might also have this problem that I could ask similar questions to?
- Can I follow up with you if I have more questions?

Thanks to Mike Fishbein,
author of Customer Development for Entrepreneurs, *for these questions.*

CONSULT *THE ENTREPRENEUR'S GUIDE TO CUSTOMER DEVELOPMENT*, CHAPTER 8 FOR MORE INFORMATION ON THE STEPS TO CUSTOMER DEVELOPMENT:

a. Business model hypotheses
b. Finding prospects
c. Reaching out to prospects
d. Engaging prospects
e. Problem-solving it

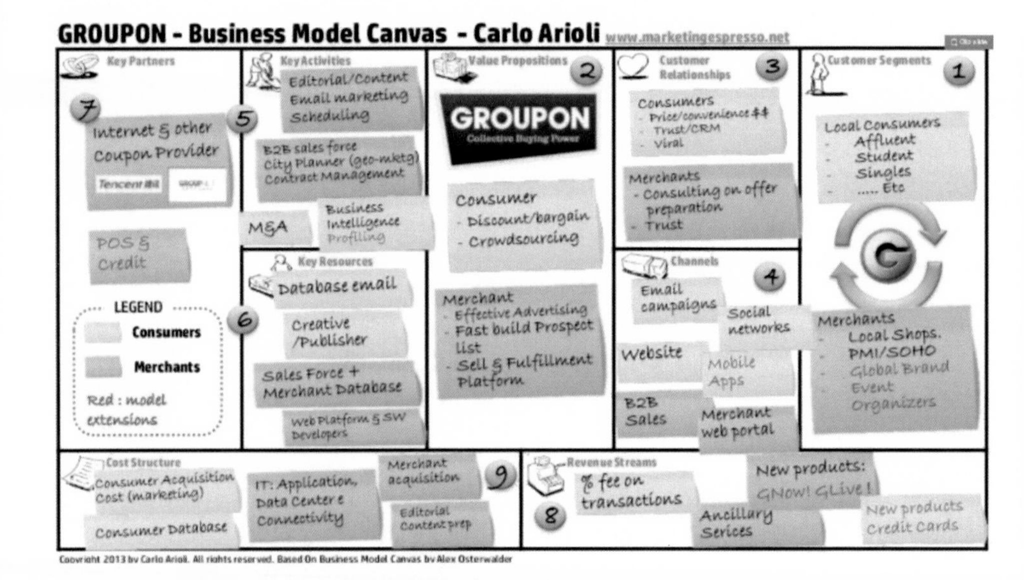

Courtesy of Carlo Arioli (2013).

FROM PROBLEM TO SOLUTION USING CDM

The assumptions you make about target markets are only guesses. Get in front of customers, ask for feedback, and analyze their problems. As you evaluate your core assumptions, some are proven wrong, and the customer guides you to a solution to their problem. Segment the customer (learn their demographics), discover their problem (needs, most time-consuming task), validate their problem (an explanation of the difficult process), ask questions to generate ideas (what are you doing now), validate your solution (what you use), and optimize the product (others with the same problem).

- Problem – Difficulty, hurdle, bad situation, identify top three problems you're addressing
- Solution – Answer, resolution, quick fix via hypothesis (untested guesses)
- Customer – Segment customers, users of the product or service
- Value – What is the unique value proposition, the primary reason you are different?
- MVP – What is the minimum feature set that demonstrates the unique value?
- Activity – What is the key action users take to revenue generation?

- Channels – Both free and paid outlets that can be used to reach the customer
- Streams – Identify the revenue model and life, gross margin, and break-even point
- Advantage – Identify something that cannot be copied or bought, an unfair advantage
- Test – Examination, research, try out via MVP assumptions
- Pivot – Change, adjust, revolve around center by funneling assumptions

Customer Development

The Four Steps to the Epiphany

Successful Strategies for Products that Win

Steve Blank

http://bit.ly/3oardD

Continuous cycle of customer interaction:

- **Rapid hypothesis testing about market, pricing, customers,...**
- **Extreme low cost, low burn, tight focus**
- **Measurable gates for investors**

Adapted from *The Startup Owner's Manual*, Steve Blank (2012, 31–39).

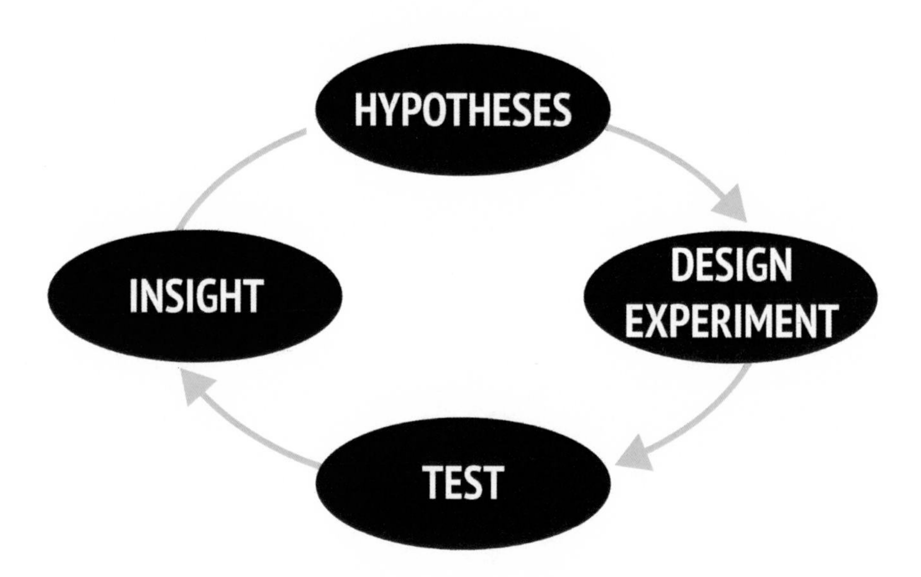

The Build-Measure-Learn loop emphasizes speed as a critical ingredient to product development. A team or company's effectiveness is determined by its ability to ideate, quickly build an MVP of that idea, measure its effectiveness in the market, and learn from that experiment. It's a learning cycle of turning ideas into products, measuring customers' reactions and behaviors against built products, and then deciding whether to persevere or pivot the idea. This process repeats as many times as necessary.

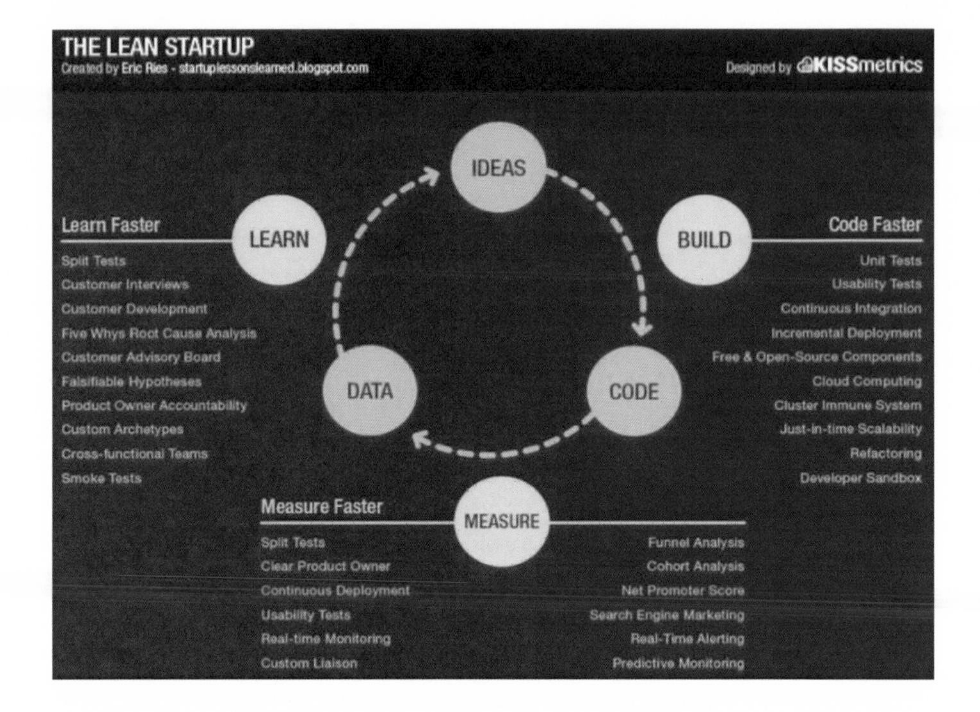

Adapted from *The Lean Startup*, Eric Ries (2011).

How to Make Customer Development Work for You:

- Find customers
- Conduct customer interviews—structure CD interviews in three parts: people, problems, and solution
- Interpret responses and make decisions

USE OF THE BUSINESS MODEL CANVAS (BMC)

***Business Model Generation*,**
Alexander Osterwalder and Yves Pigneur

This book contains tested tools for understanding, designing, reworking, and implementing business models. It uses the BMC as a strategic tool to develop new business models by describing a product's value proposition, infrastructure, customers, and finances. Released in 2010 and based on Osterwalder's earlier thesis on business model ontology, it illustrates potential trade-offs and helps align planning activities by using nine building blocks.

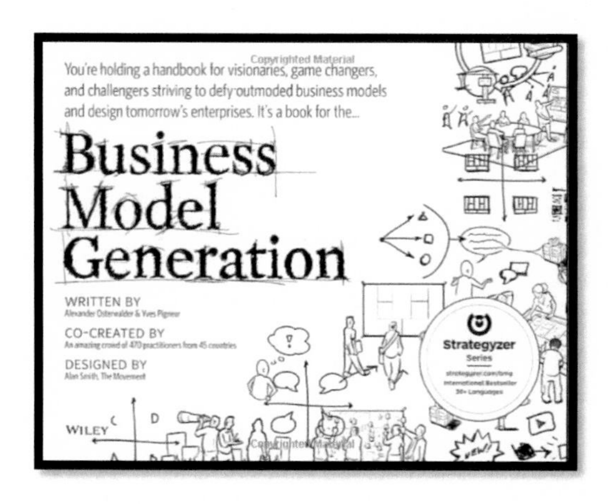

Business Model Generation, Osterwalder and Pigneur (2010).

Value Proposition Design, Osterwalder and Pigneur (2014).

The follow-up 2014 book was *Value Proposition Design.*

At the start of a new venture, the business model is unknown unless it will be a replicate of an established model (like a plumber, pharmacist, baker, etc.). Even known models have to be iterated or tweaked in some fashion to create a competitive advantage. The main purpose of the BMC is to test the idea as a hypothesis as entrepreneurs search to validate their idea until use of the canvas finds one that is repeatable and scalable:

1. Customer segments.* Who are the customers? What do they think, see, feel, and do?
2. Value propositions.* What's compelling about the proposition? Why do customers buy and use it?
3. Channels. How are the propositions promoted, sold, and delivered? Why, and is it working?

4. Customer relationships. How do you interact with the customers through their journey?
5. Revenue streams. How does the business earn revenue from the value proposition?
6. Key activities. What strategic things does the business do to deliver its proposition?
7. Key resources. What strategic assets must the business have to compete?
8. Key partnerships. What can the company not do so it can focus on its key activities?
9. Cost structure. What are the business's major cost drivers, and how are they linked to revenue?

*The so-called product/market fit is equal to a product, its benefits (what it does), features (how it works), and the experience (what it feels like to use it), and the customer, their wants (what emotions drive purchasing), needs (what are hidden needs), and fears (risks of switching to the product). The value proposition canvas allows a startup to better describe the hypotheses underlying the product/market fit. It provides assistance matching customer needs, determining the jobs to be done, and solving their problems. A good fit satisfies a strong market demand by early adopters from whom entrepreneurs gather feedback and gauge interest.

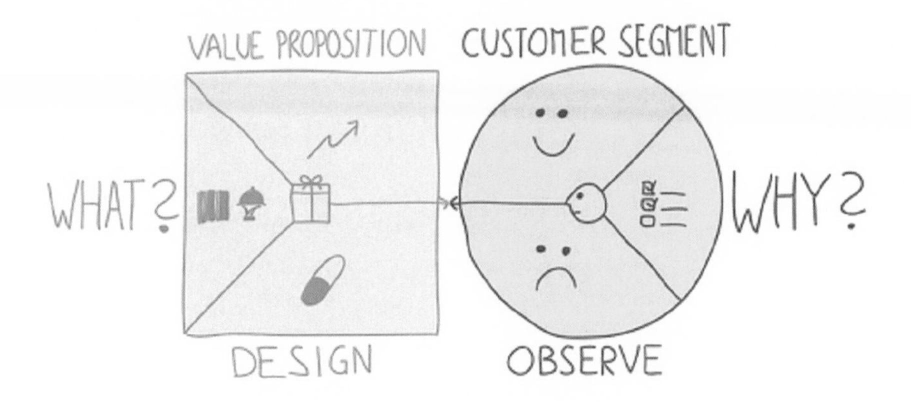

Adapted from *The Startup Owner's Manual*,
Steve Blank and Bob Dorf (2012).

Value Proposition Canvas

The experience involves customer psychology, or how the customer feels. The emotional reasons why people buy your product is dealt with in agile engineering. The product focuses less on "pains" and more on "gains," the wants that pull our hearts. The value proposition canvas helps entrepreneurs map, think, discuss, test, and pivot the product in relation to customer needs.

MECHANICS OF THE BMC:

1. Make your assumptions/hypotheses clear, explicit, and visible.
2. Explore each block, especially the first five, for creative new options and alternatives. Don't just "do it the way it's always been done."
3. The right side of the canvas is the customer-facing/customer-impact side. Customers will see and notice what you do.
4. The left side of the canvas is the infrastructure of the venture—what you will need to put in place so you can deliver your value proposition to your customer segment(s).
5. If you don't have an answer for each cell, go with what you know, then figure out the rest as it becomes more visible and important to you.
6. Use only key words and terms to fill out each cell—do not try to write a term paper.
7. Remember that this is a perpetually moving target—it is NOT a "one and done" thing. As you learn more, you will update and revise your canvas. Keep old copies so you can trace your journey.

BUSINESS MODEL CANVAS:

Written by Nik Rokop
Industry Assistant Professor of Entrepreneurship, Stuart School of Business

1. What is the Business Model Canvas (BMC)?

The BMC is a tool that gives a one-page visual snapshot of a business, an idea for a business, or a project that is exploring if it can become a business.

This version is based on the Business Model Canvas developed by Alex Osterwalder[1] (which is open source, and allowed to be modified and used). I have modified it based on my experience with very early stage ideas and first time users. I have listed questions and guidelines to help you.

It is a dynamic document, rarely a final product. Proper use of the BMC will produce a series of documents tracing the steps of a business idea, with its goal of getting to "product market fit" as defined by Marc Andreesen.[2]

2. How to Begin the BMC.

a. Define Your Customer and Problem

The best practice is to begin in the top row, filling in the "Customer" (top right) and "Problem" (top left) fields and work in towards the center.

At the beginning of your project, you may have several customers and users in mind, along with several problems and solutions. You can use the BMC to list them all initially, but to proceed further, you must choose ONE customer (or user) and ONE problem that you will solve, and use a different BMC for each set. If you try to fill out a BMC for more than one at a time, the tool will become too confusing and complicated.

b. Describe Your Solution

For each Customer and Problem set, you will have a Solution. This can be a product, service, or combination, either a prototype or ready for market.

c. Develop a Value Proposition

You begin by stating your initial "Value Proposition," which will list the benefits your solution provides to the Customer with the Problem. A good template for a value proposition is in another section of the IPRO 397 manual.* This is an external facing statement and what you will use to talk to prospective customers.

* IPRO 397 refers to the Inter-professional Projects Program at Illinois Institute of Technology's Stuart School of Business developed by Nik Rokop to showcase the work by over 120 teams in his Venture Creation course.

d. List Your Customer Channels

You will list ways you can find and reach more customers or users that you intend to satisfy with your Solution.

e. State Your Unfair Advantage

For the second row, center, create an internal facing statement, usually used to evaluate whether a solution or venture is sustainable over time. This does not need to be filled out initially, but if it exists, will give confidence to the team to continue.

f. Key Metrics for Customer or User

For the second row, right hand side, you need to develop simple, meaningful ways to measure how many customers you are engaging. How do you know you are satisfying them? How much is this increasing over time? Research businesses similar to yours and understand what they are measuring. This will be the most difficult part of building your venture, and crucial to your success.

g. Key Metrics of Your Solution

For the second row, left-hand side, the simple way to fill this out is to list all activities, goods, and organizations that you need in order to provide your solution to your customer.

From that list, you can develop some measures to let you know if you can provide your product or service in an effective way to all your customers as you grow.

h. Costs to Provide Your Solution
For the third row, left-hand side, you will quantify your costs based on the information in the "Key Metrics of Your Solution". Depending on your business model, a formula might be in the form of "unit cost" to manufacture. It will include payment you might make to partners, sales agents, cost of goods, overhead, and value of your time. These numbers will form the basis for the "Costs" and "Expenses" side of your financial projections.

i. How Much Revenue Can You Generate?
For the third row, right-hand side, you will quantify how much your customer will pay you for your product or service, how much revenue you can generate monthly or annually, and what income you generate from other sources. These numbers will form the basis of the "Revenue" side of your financial projections.

3. How to Use the BMC.

The first time you fill out the BMC, you will have the basis for creating a series of hypotheses to test. Begin by asking yourself what is the most critical hypothesis, that if proven wrong, will invalidate your business, or if proven correct, will allow you to move forward with confidence.

The IPRO 397 manual provides a good framework to test hypotheses using "Prototyping."

The "lean startup" process references below will guide you through a series of steps and provide examples that will be similar to many instances in your project.[3,4]

Keep it simple! Choose your most critical hypothesis, create a valid, testable experiment that will yield meaningful data, and use that data to fill out a new version of the BMC, incorporating any new insights and information you have.

Repeat this process for each customer/problem set, and over time you will have a rich record of the development of your venture with enough valid data to make decisions on which direction you should take.[5]

References:

1. Alex Osterwalder, Business Model Generation: http://www.businessmodelgeneration.com/
2. Product Market Fit: http://web.stanford.edu/class/ee204/ProductMarketFit.html
3. Ash Maurya: http://leanstack.com/
4. Steve Blank: http://steveblank.com/
5. Javelin Board: https://www.youtube.com/watch?v=F-5Iyj9A1MU

BUSINESS MODEL CANVAS

WHAT IS YOUR SOLUTION? WHO IS YOUR CUSTOMER or USER?

<table>
<tr>
<td>PROBLEM

What Customer or User problem are you trying to solve?</td>
<td>SOLUTION

Your PRODUCT or SERVICE</td>
<td colspan="2">Value Proposition to the Customer or User (Pitch)

Single, clear, compelling message that tells what problem you are solving, for whom, and how you are solving it.</td>
<td>CHANNELS

How do you find them?

Do you need partners?</td>
<td>CUSTOMER or USER

Who pays you?

Be specific and concrete.</td>
</tr>
<tr>
<td colspan="2">Key Metrics of your SOLUTION
Main things you measure

How are you delivering your solution?

Who is building your solution? Do you have subcontractors? Partners?</td>
<td colspan="2">Your Unfair Advantage

What specific insights and/or expertise do you have that give you an advantage over your competitors?</td>
<td colspan="2">Key Metrics of your CUSTOMER or USER
Main things you measure

How many are there?

What do they look like? PERSONAS

How do you know you are solving their problems?</td>
</tr>
<tr>
<td colspan="3">What does it cost to provide your solution?

What does it cost to find customers or users? How do you find them? Do you pay sales commissions?
What does it cost to deliver your solution?
- People (are you paying yourself?)
- Materials (what are you using to build your solution?)
- Purchases (computers, TV ads)
- Are you trading for services?</td>
<td colspan="3">Who pays you? How much Revenue can you generate?

Is the person you are serving paying you?
Are you getting support from donors?
Are you getting grants from the government?</td>
</tr>
</table>

Nik Rokop, Illinois Institute of Technology
Stuart School of Business (2015).

The Marketing Plan

A marketing plan covers activities directed toward an exchange intended to satisfy human needs or wants. It describes the marketing strategies the business will use to influence customers to purchase their product or service. It employs the "four Ps" of a marketing mix: price, product, place, and promotion. Among considerations for price are competition, demand, product establishment, and best mode to reach the desired customer.

Three considerations when marketing a small business startup are selection of a target market, deciding how to segment that market, and creating a unique position within it. A target must be attractive, and a company has to have the ability to meet its demand. By focusing on a specific trade or niche you can become an expert. Use your skills and background to mesh with the target, and, if necessary, acquire an expertise to serve it and talk its language.

Try applying the market segmentation method within the market, geographic (population by location), demographic (gender, income, age, etc.), psychographic (lifestyle differences such as opinion, politics, etc.), and behavioral (observations, price attractiveness, etc.). With limited resources you may choose to target only one or two segments of the whole market and find the growth space inside the market.

You'll want to develop a marketing plan based on your vision and analysis of the customer. A plan is based on research both primary (CD) and secondary, and nothing replaces the importance of customer development as used in lean startup and agile development. Let the end user determine the specifics for your service or product based on what they tell you they want to have to satisfy their needs.

Think competitive advantage as you plan. What distinguishes your product or service in the mind of your target market and provides the difference they want to have? It's hard to beat the old-fashioned "four Ps" when looking for a competitive advantage. Meet a customer need, price the product low enough to sell but high enough to make a profit, choose a location that reaches the target best, and promote its popularity by any means that reach the end user. Publicity is free and great.

Choose your target segment carefully because with limited resources you want to be as well aligned with the market as possible. As you test your ideas with a potential customer, it may be necessary to redefine your target according to what the customer tells you will or will not work. Use the nine-section BMC to find the right product/market fit and sweet spots for profit, resources, selling channels, and key activities. Above all, build a brand through any of the following: logo, name, reputation, personality, ethical standards, treating employees well, association with charity, and active community involvement.

AGILE ENGINEERING

—*The Lean Startup* by Eric Ries

This book is a scientific approach to creating and managing startups. In it, you can see how to get a desired product into customers' hands faster. The book teaches how to drive a startup, how to steer and turn, and when to persevere and grow a business with maximum acceleration. It is a principled approach to new product research, and a primary reference for agile development.

In agile development, user stories are used to convey what the customer wants. A good user story follows the format of a typical user who wants to do something to reach a desired benefit. Bill Wake, a good writer of agile thought, recommends the acronym

INVEST—independent, negotiable, valuable, estimable, small, and testable. The best example of agile development is the story of Uber.[3]

Eric Ries added the psychology of collaborative teamwork based on his software development experience. He knew solutions evolved by using cross-functional teams. Use of agile engineering planning is adaptive, improvements are continuous, and changes are made rapidly. It was developed in the 1990s as an improvement over the slower "waterfall-oriented" (sequential design) method. Agile engineering responds to change instead of following a plan, collaborates with customers rather than negotiates a contract, and stresses individual interaction over process and tools.

Ries places customer development at the front end of the agile process and made "big room planning" with Sharpie, tape, Post-its, and markers the norm. His agility is a top-down process done by teams formed to accomplish the idea for a product. Collaboration is deliberately noisy and confrontational, but outcomes are creative improvement. "Synergy" best describes the innovation and creativity that results from teamwork.

---

[3] Mohamed Amine Belarbi, "Startup from the Bottom: Here is How Uber Started Out," Gulf Elite, published July 14, 2014, http://gulfelitemag.com/startup-bottom-uber-started/. In 2008 two friends visiting a conference in Paris had trouble finding a taxi. They were already brainstorming how to find cars at the right place and time. By 2010 they had tested a few black cars in New York City, and soon thereafter disrupted ride sharing forever.

DISCIPLINED ENTREPRENEURSHIP

by Bill Aulet, Director, MIT Entrepreneurship

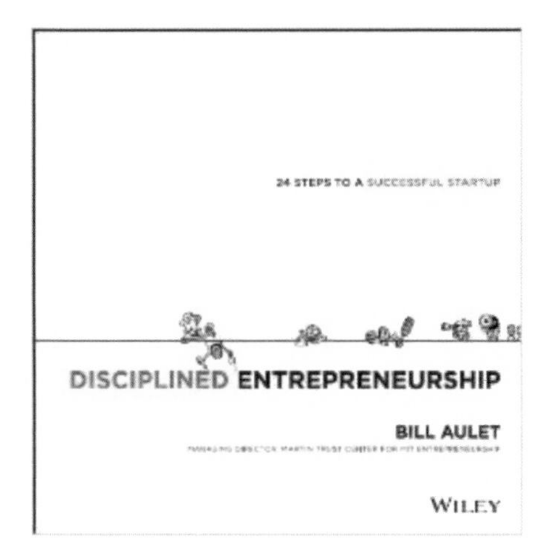

This book, written in 2013, is a refinement to lean startup written by one of the USA's best entrepreneurship professors, Bill Aulet, managing director of the Martin Trust Center for MIT entrepreneurship. A former pro basketball player and senior lecturer in MIT's Sloan School of Management, Bill has built on the lean startup base using thinking from *Crossing the Chasm*, *Blue Ocean Strategy*, experimentation work by Stefan Thomke, and primary market research/basic competitive strategy to design his own version of evidence-based, new-venture startup. In his twenty-four steps to a successful startup, Bill argues entrepreneurship can be taught, it is a team sport, and ideas are less important than a team's ability to execute in a focused manner.

Disciplined Entrepreneurship can change the way you think about starting a company. The book shows how to create a successful startup through developing an innovative product. It breaks down the necessary processes into an integrated, comprehensive, and proven twenty-four-step framework that any industrious person can learn and apply. Because entrepreneurship is a sequential process, Bill starts from the most logical point, a "beachhead" market, and "snakes" through to a product/services plan twenty-four steps later.

Disciplined Entrepreneurship, Bill Aulet (2013).

His steps are based on six themes: (1) who is your customer, (2) what can you do for your customer, (3) how does your customer acquire your product, (4) how do you make money off your product, (5) how do you design and build your product, and (6) how do you scale your business? His belief is we have a crisis in storytelling, and successful entrepreneurship requires the "spirit of a pirate" combined with "skills of a Navy Seal." *Disciplined Entrepreneurship* focuses on the IDE (inspiration-driven entrepreneurship) versus the SME (small-to-medium enterprise) and is value-based versus credential-centric. Strength comes from the heterogeneity of the team and cross-functional enterprise. The process is not any one tool, but rather a combined toolbox. It might be the preferred method for developing a new product model.

WHO IS YOUR CUSTOMER?

1. Market segmentation
2. Select a beachhead market
3. Build an end-user profile
4. Calculate the TAM size for the beachhead market
5. Profile the persona for the beachhead market
9. Identify your next customers

WHAT CAN YOU DO FOR YOUR CUSTOMER?

6. Full life cycle use case
7. High-level product specification
8. Quantify the value proposition
10. Define your Core
11. Chart your competitive position

HOW DOES YOUR CUSTOMER ACQUIRE YOUR PRODUCT?

12. Determine the customer's decision-making unit (DMU)
13. Map the process to acquire a paying customer
18. Map the sales process to acquire a customer

HOW DO YOU MAKE MONEY OFF YOUR PRODUCT?

15. Design a business model
16. Set your priding framework
17. Calculate the lifetime value of an acquired customer (LTV)
19. Calculate the cost of customer acquisition (COCA)

HOW DO YOU DESIGN & BUILD YOUR PRODUCT?

20. Identify key assumptions
21. Test key assumptions
22. Define the minimum viable business product (MVBP)
23. Show that "the dogs will eat the dog food"

HOW DO YOU SCALE YOUR BUSINESS?

14. Calculate the TAM size for follow-on markets
24. Develop a product plan

24 Steps. 6 Themes

Disciplined Entrepreneurship, Bill Aulet (2013).

Unlike normal lean startup that relies on the BMC (business model canvas) tool, it is easier to formulate a vision and mission statement so entrepreneurs don't get bogged down with overbearing "to-do" lists. Disciplined Entrepreneurship (DE) provides better guidance for uncertainty, a method for client activity, specific directions, concrete ideas, and provides more follow-through. It can be combined with the Lean LaunchPad method to validate hypotheses. The entrepreneur learns sooner rather than later if their idea is a good one. DE serves as a roadmap to the BMC and leads a wannabe entrepreneur to the product/market fit through a heavy focus on the value proposition and customer segment. It stresses communication and sales skills to facilitate early customer interaction and mentor engagement.

VALUE CAPTURE—
THE LEAN PRODUCT PLAYBOOK

by Dan Olsen

This book explains how to innovate via MVPs and rapid customer feedback. It is how to build products customers want by determining your target customer, identifying underserved customer needs, defining your value proposition, specifying your MVP feature set, creating your MVP prototype, and testing your MVP repeatedly with customers. *The Lean Product Playbook* is a valuable component in the lean startup process with its own hierarchy of needs similar to Maslow's human needs. Olsen calls his hierarchy the product/market fit pyramid with five layers—the target customers on bottom, followed by underserved needs next. Then, before the three forming the product at the top, he inserts the product/market (P/M) fit as a third layer with the value proposition next, topped by the user experience he calls "UX."

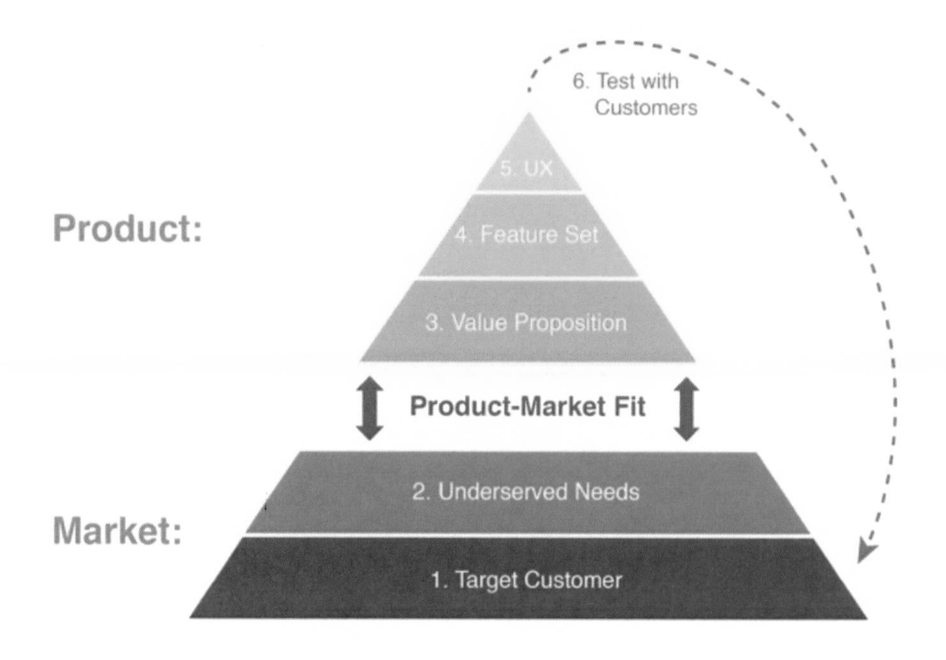

The Lean Product Playbook, Dan Olsen (2015).

It is the UX design (the value proposition) formed into a P/M fit that captures value. Entrepreneurs can use the principles of UX design to iteratively improve the P/M fit to build great products. *The Lean Product Playbook*'s sole aim is to create products that customers love. Olsen has the design iterate through the hypothesize-test-learn loop with additional waves of user testing to achieve higher and higher levels of P/M fit. He can visualize return on investment by the customer value created. Using waves of iteration, the entrepreneur eventually gets to a P/M fit and perseveres or pivots. Details in his book allow measurement of each test wave to see how many users give the same feedback expressed as a percentage.

The point is to get objective feedback from real customers. He recommends starting by asking questions about their current behavior and feelings about the key benefit you plan to provide, and to ask open versus closed questions ("why," "how," and "what"), allowing plenty of latitude in answering. MVP focuses the customer at the top of the lean product pyramid. It's basically the minimum amount of functionality the target customer considers viable. When you are building a process rather than a product, the MVP becomes "minimum viable feature." What needs does the end user have that your product or process can satisfy?

SUBTOPICS

Comparison of Methodologies

On the next page is a comparison of three lean startup philosophies based on six categories: hypotheses, validation, market exploration, how they build to solution, how they validate the solution, and their go-to-market strategy. Both Ries and Furr-Ahlstrom were published in 2011 while Blank's first book, *The Four Steps to the Epiphany*, was published in 2003 (subsequent book *The Startup Owner's Manual* in 2012).

	Furr & Ahlstrom	Blank	Ries
Create the hypothesis	Develop a hypothesis about the problem. Then develop a big idea hypothesis including features of the solution and whom to sell it to. Be careful with specific features in the solution. The problem should be a big one to the customers.	Include detailed information about the product, but also about the market, competition, and distribution	Create two kinds of hypotheses: the value and growth hypotheses. They establish whether the solution delivers value to the customers and how the customers get information about the product/service.
Validate the problem	Focus mainly on low-end customers. Use the response rate on emails or cold calls to measure the magnitude of the problem (at least 50% to move on). It is important to be aware of the type of customer the person contacted is.	Start with a long list of potential customers. The initial purpose is to find customers that share your vision. The title of the customer is not the important thing. You should focus on understanding the customer's needs.	Validate it together with the solution.
Exploration of the market attractiveness	Perform a quick exploration of market dynamics and competition after validating the problem. Check the size, growth, and competition, but also if the technological cycle of the market is ready for adapting the new technology.	Gather a vast amount of knowledge about the market, ranging from quantitative data, like market size and growth, to qualitative, like trends and needs.	Interact with mainstream customers to understand if there is a problem to solve and thus an attractive market.
Build the solution	Develop a minimum feature set based on data from previous stages and by contacting customers. Use a rapid prototyping technology to build and test, respectively, a virtual prototype and solution. Focus on few features that will drive the purchase and simplify.	Start with a hypothesis of the product features, and then validate them before finally building a prototype.	Create an MVP to test the hypotheses. It is the simplest way to start validated learning. Try to simplify with few features. The prototype should build upon the riskiest assumptions that need to be verified.
Validate the solution	Use an iterative process to validate the three consecutive steps. Use interview guides to learn about the problem, how it is solved today, and opinions about the proposed solution. In the solution test, the whole buying panel should be involved.	Validate the features of the product and the business model with the customers. Then build the product based on the features, and the validation is the sales to the earlyvangelists.	Test the MVP on early adopters in an iterative process, where it is continuously developed to better fit their needs. The data should be quantified and evaluated to track the progress.
Go-to market strategy	Collect information about the different types of customers in the buying panel and their needs. Also try to understand the players between your company and the customers and exploit them to succeed.	Use a hypothesis about the business mdel that is to be verified. Should also investigate e.g. distribution channels, sales materials, and sales road maps.	Ries does not focus on the players between the company and the customers.

Implementing Lean Startup Methodology,
Jonas Qvillberg and Anders Gustafsson (2012).

Concept of Pains and Gains

Two components of the BMC, the value proposition and the customer segment, help the entrepreneur project the best way the business idea can solve the problems, difficulties, and needs of customers. Jobs gather the customer needs, problems, and tasks the business is trying to perform; customer pains gather the negative emotions, undesired costs, and risk. Gains add value to the customer. The premise is for the canvas to inspire solutions. A value proposition canvas (see page 36) offers an easy-to-understand overview of what a customer needs and why.

In his book *The Lean Product Playbook*, Dan Olsen uses Quicken as an example. At the time cofounders Scott Cook and Tom Proulx launched, there were dozens of personal-finance products on the market. After research, they concluded none of them achieved product/market fit. The customer was expressing many pains and an inability to balance their checkbooks, track their balances, and see where their money went. By talking to customers they made sure Quicken addressed those needs. The customer pain points were adequately met and turned into valuable gains.

Integration of a Business Plan

Many new businesses are traditional and begin with an iteration of a known business model. Take the plumber who works for a master for several years, buys his own truck, and goes out on his own. His primary focus is creating a competitive advantage over other plumbers to build his own clientele.

1. Cost, speed, product offering, distribution network, customer support

2. Differential advantage is when the product or service seems better than competitors'

3. Some differentiations are benefits: location, price, operational method, and goodwill

4. Make the advantage sustainable and always examine direct competitors

If iterating a known business model, use the BMC to refine your differentiation. Make sure the end user values the competitive advantage until the point of viability or sustainability. Then switch to a traditional business plan when sustainable, as below.

New Venture Financing Cycle

At some point the startup is viable. It has achieved demand, sustainability, and is now scalable. Usually sometime during the second stage of the startup financing cycle, it becomes apparent the idea is working and the product or service can be ramped up. Funds can be committed, staff expanded, and marketing engaged.

Startup Financing Cycle

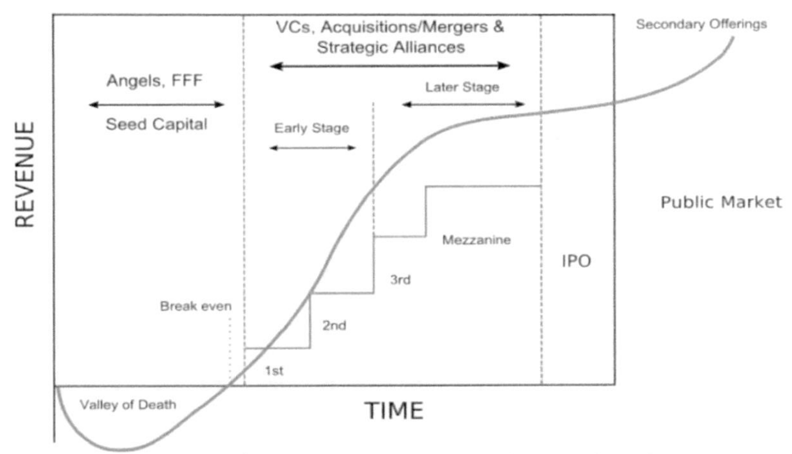

Somewhere in the 1st or 2nd ladder of the Early Stage the hypothesis has been proven, and the product can be scaled (i. e., growth will be sustained). At that point a traditional business plan is needed.

The Entrepreneurial S-Curve, Mary Han (2005).

Sustainability is the ability to survive long enough to generate a return on investment, and scalability is the ability for a business to grow faster than costs. Once a startup has reached sustainability, it's appropriate to write a traditional business plan for second-stage funding requests (bank lenders, equity partners) so that the company develops standard operating procedures. This document can now focus on knowns, and the BMC serves as an outline for it.

Business plans written at this stage are more specific. Competition, target markets, product characteristics, pricing, promotion direction, and ways of distribution are easier to forecast. The mission statement is clear and concise, taken directly from a refined BMC. Demographics, keys to success, management requirements, ownership structure, a break-even analysis, and valuation of intellectual property are all easier to describe at a point of sustainability. Testing is over, and the market demand is established.

EXAMPLES OF LEAN STARTUP SUCCESS

Dropbox

Files from anywhere shared with anyone.

Wealthfront

Personalized investment profiles (asset allocation, risk assessment, and taxes).

Grockit

Online learning platform for test preparation (SAT, LSAT, etc.).

IMVU

Social media in 3-D to meet new people, chat, and play games.

Votizen

First social lobbying platform whose tools led to a US Senate bill.

Aardvark

Social search engine acquired by Google (which answers subjective questions).

Uber

Founder Travis Kalanick interviewed existing "black car drivers" for interest in his concept.

Zappos

Online retailer, now part of Amazon (MVP = buy shoes online) with best service and best selection.

Student example – Professor Andy Gold of Hillsborough Community College coached a student through declinations from smaller restaurants for a substitute chef. Andy recommended higher-end restaurants, and the student was about to give up when one owner/operator mentioned his sister ran a catering business and did have a need. She jumped on the idea as a widespread want, and our lean startup student found a demand and established a major service to the catering industry.

WHERE EVIDENCE-BASED SUCCEEDS AND BUSINESS PLANS FAIL

1. Upgrading. Model often starts with an idea to improve or disrupt an already successful product or service and make it better.

2. Less paperwork. The process of using the BMC, a nine-block template laid out on a single page, allows the founder to validate an idea using live interactions with target customers.

3. Builds integrated feedback. Canvas supports continuous feedback in a loop that validates the customer's views about a hypothesis. By conducting at least one hundred interviews, assumptions are changed to facts.

4. Timing is everything. Lean startup does not commit to a full production version of the product until the target customer is satisfied enough that they are willing to prepay and order the new product or service, i.e., the demand is real.

Investment Readiness Level

10. Product market validation
9. High fidelity MVP
8. Validated two or more marketing channels
7. $ earned
6. Low fidelity MVP
5. Problem solution validation
4. Market sizing and competittive analysis
3. Identify and interview first customer
2. First pass lean canvas
1. Vision clearly and briefly articulated

Steve Blank, "How Investors Make Better Decisions: The Investment Readiness Level."

"The Lean Startup Method teaches you how to drive a startup: how to steer, when to turn, and when to persevere and grow a business with maximum acceleration."

Steve Blank, "Is This Startup Ready for Investment?"

OTHER IMPORTANT MODEL DISCOVERY BOOKS

Customer Development for Entrepreneurs: How to Test Startup Ideas and Build Products People Love by Mike Fishbein

Mike validated and launched three new consumer technology products, advises Fortune 500 companies, and is the founder of stpcollege.com in New York City. He is an expert in customer development, lean product strategy, and customer acquisition. The book is a perfect complement to *Lean Startup* by Eric Ries.

The Art of the Start by Guy Kawasaki

Advice about innovation, recruitment, fund-raising, and branding. Version 2.0 updates the original with the latest insights and practical advice about social media, how to build a strong team, face down competition, and focus on what is important. Kawasaki was chief evangelist at Apple, teaches at UC Berkeley, and has decades of startup experience.

Just Start by Leonard Schlesinger and Charles Kiefer (Babson)

Written by Babson College professors, this book outlines their Creaction* version of lean startup. It relies on ETA, or entrepreneurial thought in action. Before taking any action, answer four questions: Is it feasible? Is it worth doing? Does a market exist? Do I want to do it? Then you take action, gain additional insights, and build on what you learn.

*Creaction is Babson College's term for lean startup, which they define as entrepreneurial thought and action (ETA) or getting started and adjust along the way (Schlesinger and Kiefer 2012, 131).

Lean Customer Development by Cindy Alvarez

Build products your customers will buy. How to validate product and company ideas through customer development research before you waste months and millions on a product or service no one needs or wants. Provides open-ended interviews and fast, flexible research techniques to learn the problems customers need to solve.

Running Lean by Ash Maurya

Iterate from Plan A to a plan that works. Most products fail not because they can't be completed, but because we waste time, money, and effort building the wrong product. The promise of *Running Lean* is a systematic process for quickly vetting a product and raising the odds of success.

All In Startup by Diana Kander

Launching a new idea when everything is on the line told as a novel. The beautiful Samantha provides a lifeline for entrepreneurs thinking about launching a new idea or for those who have already started but can't generate traction. The answer is a new scientific method for innovation (a.k.a. lean startup).

The E-Myth Revisited by Michael E. Gerber

This book tells you that assumptions get in the way of running a small business. Gerber applies systems and the lessons of franchising to any business whether or not a franchise. This book enables an entrepreneur to grow their business in a predictable and productive way.

Getting to Plan B by John Mullins and Randy Komisar

How to change plans in real time as challenges arise. This book is the handbook for an entrepreneur's adapted mindset, and it suggests moves required to lead a company in today's ever-changing world. Mullins and Komisar challenge and redefine how organizational strategy and innovation should be managed. Presents an understanding of what it takes to drive an early-stage company to success. *Getting to Plan B* is about the mindset and changes required to lead a company through change when Plan A doesn't work. It depends on data gathering and continual market evaluation.

Nail It Then Scale It by Nathan Furr and Paul Ahlstrom

Nail It Then Scale It helps entrepreneurs through the process of launching a high-growth company. It includes not high-level principles, but a step-by-step guide of key actions successful entrepreneurs take to reduce risk and increase success. The book answers key questions including why most new businesses fail, what first steps successful entrepreneurs take, and descriptions of the most common failure traps to avoid.

Entrepreneurship

The Lean LaunchPad

Taught by Steve Blank

UDACITY

Udacity online course[4] (approx. 1 month)

Silicon Valley tech firms like Google, Facebook, and Cloudera built an online training course, one of which is "How to Build a Startup," the Lean LaunchPad. It introduces the customer development process by Steve Blank, who also hosts several videos. Its main idea is to rapidly develop and test ideas by gathering large quantities of customer feedback. Steve Blank provides insight into the key steps needed to build a successful startup. It is part of the ULS Course Map on p. 81.

[4] Steve Blank and Kathleen Mullaney, "How to Build a Startup: The Lean LaunchPad," Udacity, https://www.udacity.com/course/how-to-build-a-startup--ep245.

Tim O'Reilly, http://www.oreilly.com/tim/

Tim O'Reilly started as a technical writer who published computer manuals. After the dot-com bust, he was a key figure in the web renaissance, focusing on the role of data rather than software in driving competitive advantage. His writings and speeches have played a key role in understanding human values and use of the internet.

THE ULS* COURSE MAP

By Clinton E. Day, Entrepreneurship Adjunct Professor

*Understanding Lean Startup

Mindset – Read *All In Startup* by Diane Kander (sixth in list above) to see the utility of using an evidence-based entrepreneurship method and a launch vs. a business plan.
Understand Why

Videos – Register for the free "How to Build a Startup" course on Udacity at https://www.udacity.com/courses/ep245 and use eight lessons online.
Nuts & Bolts

Simulation – Register on Venture Blocks for "The Nanu Challenge," a game-like exercise to help planning. http://ventureblocks.com/#home
Customer Need

Canvas – Register on Launch Plan for use of the site as the business model canvas (BMC) tool on which to develop

over time a viable product or service that has a demand in a market. http://www.launchplan.com/

Build Value

Mentor – Select a mentor from a small business or professional advisor to assist you through the process (friend, entrepreneur, SCORE chapter, SBDC) and connect with a qualified entrepreneurship instructor (course, workforce agency, community college, incubator) willing to act as an advisor from time to time.

Two Advisors

Adjust – Do not be afraid of failure or change, as both are part of the lean startup process. A target market segment will guide you through feedback of what works and what does not. Listening carefully will lead an entrepreneur to a viable product/service, which solves a problem, satisfies a need, and can then be scaled.

Design Certainty

NEW VENTURE DISCOVERY

Divide the process into weeks. Watch an Udacity video each week (two times), become familiar with the Launch Plan software, and allow advisors to view changes to the BMC each week by printing a copy to share and record. Mentoring works only when the entrepreneur respects the time of the advisor, preschedules, arrives on time, and does the work. Each week the student refines the nine sections of the BMC by asking special, open-ended questions designed to bring forth the truth regarding a target's interest in an idea.

INTERVIEWING END USER

Each week the BMC improves through use of target customer interviews. Only the actual persona of the consumer has the ability to say if the idea or hypothesis is needed or can solve their problem. Working through the right side of the canvas first, each component needs to be refined as understanding increases. The best questions are open ended and invite good explanations from the customer. It is always important that the primary founder or owner-to-be does the questioning to apply their knowledge. Prepare for the buyer interview in advance. Get it on record. A good opening statement might be, "Take me back to the day . . ." Use their words to ask follow-ups, try to understand the whole story, and keep the conversation going. Make an attempt to understand the buyer's world, their jargon, and what sources they used to make decisions. Nothing is more important than the buyer's point of view.

On the right side, the most important relationship is the P/M fit, or the interaction between the value proposition and the customer segment. Until you have a good product/market fit there is no reason to go further. A value must be created for the target customer or there is no viable model to continue. This P/M fit is a product or a service, its benefits and features, and customer wants, needs, and fears. The right order for BMC work is in sequence: (1) value propositions, (2) customer segments, (3) channels, (4) customer relationships, (5) revenue streams, (6) key activities, (7) key resources, (8) key partners, and (9) cost structure.

SUMMARY ULS COURSE MAP

Components of the ULS Course Map are (1) *All In Startup* reading, (2) registration for Udacity, Nanu Challenge (Venture Blocks), and Launch Plan online, (3) eight weeks of Udacity videos and *The Startup Owner's Manual* readings*, and (4) four weeks outside conducting interviews to build the BMC through iterations, pivots, and feasibility testing.

*Readings from *The Startup Owner's Manual*, which explains the customer development process, should be broken down into twenty-five to thirty-five pages a week to correspond to the eight-week Udacity videos. It's recommended the ULS study be over a three-month period conducting Launch Plan interviews during the last month.

*Read pages from *The Startup Owner's Manual* in order during the eight weeks you watch Udacity videos: 50–75, 76–84, 84–97, 189–221, 260–266, 474, 112–125, 419–428, 98–111, 135–145, 242–244, 332–343, 406–412, 126–168, 257–272, 480–482, 180–188, 240, 266–269.

This ULS course was developed by the FGCU Institute for Entrepreneurship to train Florida veterans and active military for entrepreneurial success using a lean startup curriculum.

GLOSSARY

Agile

"Agile software development is a group of software-development methods based on iterative and incremental development, where requirements and solutions evolve through collaboration between self-organizing, cross-functional teams. It promotes adaptive planning, evolutionary development and delivery, a time-boxed iterative approach, and encourages rapid and flexible response to change. It is a conceptual framework that promotes foreseen interactions throughout the development cycle. The Agile Manifesto introduced the term in 2001." ("Agile software development," *Wikipedia*, https://en.wikipedia.org/wiki/Agile_software_development.)

Angel Investor

"An angel is a wealthy individual willing to invest in a company at its earlier stages in exchange for an ownership stake, often in the form of preferred stock or convertible debt. Angels are considered one of the oldest sources of capital for startup entrepreneurs." ("What's an Angel Investor?" *The Wall Street Journal*, published April 18, 2010, http://www.wsj.com/articles/SB10001424052702303491304575188420191459904.)

Beachhead Market

The first market your business sells in.

Burn Rate

"The rate at which a new company uses up its venture capital to finance overhead before generating positive cash flow from operations. In other words, it's a measure of negative cash flow." When your burn rate increases or revenue falls it is typically time to make decisions on expenses. ("Burn Rate," *Investopedia*, http://www.investopedia.com/terms/b/burnrate.asp - axzz1q2ALYK2G.)

Bootstrapping

"Bootstrapping or booting refers to a group of metaphors that share a common meaning: a self-sustaining process that proceeds without external help." The meaning will vary depending on context. Bootstrapping in computing and software development varies slightly from bootstrapping in business. The commonalities are the characteristics of "self-sustainability" and creating something that can be "grown." ("Bootstrapping," *Wikipedia*, https://en.wikipedia.org/wiki/Bootstrapping.)

Bootstrap Startup

"Bootstrapping involves launching a business on a low budget. Practically this means that you'll outsource (most likely off-shore) your design and development, you'll rent your servers, you won't have an office and you'll have no salary. Prior to launch, the only expensive professional services which you'll buy will be your legal advice and accountancy services. Everything else, you'll have to pick up yourself and learn as you go along." ("How to Bootstrap Your Startup," Read Write Web, http://www.readwriteweb.com/archives/how_to_bootstrap_your_startup.php [site discontinued].)

1. Ideation (Demo)
2. Valley of Death (Sell)
3. Growth (Build)

Note that a bootstrap and lean startup have differences and bootstrapping does not mean spending any money.
"Bootstrapping and Lean Startups are quite complementary. Both cover techniques for building low-burn startups by eliminating waste through the maximization of existing resources first before expending effort on the acquisition of new or external resources. While bootstrapping provides a strategic roadmap for achieving sustainability through customer funding (i.e., charging customers), lean startups provide a more tactical approach to achieving those goals through validated learning."
("Bootstrapping a Lean Startup," Ash Maurya,
https://leanstack.com/bootstrapping-a-lean-startup/
http://www.ashmaurya.com/2010/03/bootstrapping-a-lean-startup/ [site discontinued].)

Business Plan

"A business plan is a written document that describes a business, its objectives, its strategies, the market it is in and its financial forecasts. It has many functions, from securing external funding to measuring success within your business."
A business plan is a static operational document to how your business will run. ("Write a business plan," Gov.uk, last modified December 11, 2014, https://www.gov.uk/write-business-plan.)

Business Model Canvas

"The Business Model Canvas is a strategic management template for developing new or documenting existing business models. It is a visual chart with elements describing a firm's value proposition, infrastructure, customers, and finances. It assists firms in aligning their activities by illustrating potential

trade-offs." A business model is a dynamic document that describes how your company creates, delivers, and captures value.
("Business Model Canvas," *Wikipedia*,
https://en.wikipedia.org/wiki/Business_Model_Canvas.)

THE 9 BUSINESS MODEL CANVAS BUILDING BLOCKS:

1. Value Propositions
2. Customer Segments
3. Channels
4. Customer Relationships
5. Revenue Streams
6. Key Activities
7. Key Resources
8. Key Partnerships
9. Cost Structure

("The Business Model Canvas," Strategyzer,
http://www.businessmodelgeneration.com/canvas/bmc.)

Customer Development Model
"The 'traditional' way to approaching business is the Product Development Model. It starts with a product idea followed by months of building to deliver it to the public." However, the Customer Development Model begins by talking to prospective customers and developing something they are interested in purchasing/using. These concepts are promoted strongly by

Steve Blank and Eric Ries, who encourage startups to get early and frequent customer feedback before developing their products too far (in the wrong direction).

The four steps to the model
1. Customer Discovery
2. Customer Validation
3. Customer Creation
4. Company Building

("A Simple Guide to the Customer Development Model," find the tech guy, published June 16, 2011, http://findthetechguy.com/a-simple-guide-to-the-customer-development-model/.)

Disruption

"An innovation that helps create a new market and value network, and eventually goes on to disrupt an existing market and value network (over a few years or decades), displacing an earlier technology. The term is used in business and technology literature to describe innovations that improve a product or service in ways that the market does not expect, typically first by designing for a different set of consumers in the new market and later by lowering prices in the existing market." The term "disruptive technologies" was coined by Clayton M. Christensen and articulated in his book *The Innovator's Dilemma.* The term "disruption" is now often used by startups to describe any product or idea that may change existing markets or products (planned or unplanned). However, to be used correctly, it should link to Christensen's original theory. The confusion is best explained here. An example is the disruption Wikipedia caused to the encyclopedia market.

("Disruptive innovation," *Wikipedia*,
https://en.wikipedia.org/wiki/Disruptive_innovation.)

Elevator Pitch

"An elevator pitch is a concise, carefully planned, and well-practiced description about your company that your mother should be able to understand in the time it would take to ride up an elevator." Being able to pitch your idea is crucial for entrepreneurs and valuable in any formal or informal networking situation. It allows you to quickly describe your concept to anyone in a short period of time, including potential partners or investors.
("How to Write an Elevator Speech," *Business Know How*,
http://www.businessknowhow.com/money/elevator.htm.)

Entrepreneur

"An entrepreneur is an individual who accepts financial risks and undertakes new financial ventures. The word derives from the French 'entrer' (to enter) and 'prendre' (to take), and in a general sense applies to any person starting a new project or trying a new opportunity."
("What is an Entrepreneur?" wiseGEEK,
http://www.wisegeek.org/what-is-an-entrepreneur.htm.)

Equity

"In finance, equity is ownership in any asset after all debts associated with that asset are paid off." Equity equals Assets minus Liabilities. In terms of startup, it is commonly used to describe a business giving up a percentage of ownership in exchange for cash. An equity investor is then entitled to share in any future profits and/or sale of business assets (after debts are paid off).

("Equity," *Investopedia*,
http://www.investopedia.com/terms/e/equity.asp#axzz1q2ALYK2G.)

Incubator

"Business incubators are projects designed to help new businesses develop and successfully launch. In some instances, the projects are overseen by colleges or universities and are based in facilities located on campus." ("What is a Business Incubator?" wiseGEEK, http://www.wisegeek.com/what-is-a-business-incubator.htm.)
In technology circles, YC or Y Combinator is probably the most well-known incubator.
"In 2005, Y Combinator developed a new model of startup funding. Twice a year we invest a small amount of money (average $18k) in a large number of startups (most recently 65)." (Home page of Y Combinator, http://www.ycombinator.com/.)

Intraprenuer

"Coined in the 1980s by management consultant Gifford Pinchot, intrapreneurs are used by companies that are in great need of new, innovative ideas. Today, instead of waiting until the company is in a bind, most companies try to create an environment where employees are free to explore ideas. If the idea looks profitable, the person behind it is given an opportunity to become an intrapreneur." "Intrapreneurs" hold many similar characteristics to "Entrepreneurs" and may well leave their jobs to pursue a career as an entrepreneur. Companies seek out intrapreneurs to effect change within their organizations.
("Intrapreneur," *Investopedia*,
http://www.investopedia.com/terms/i/intrapreneur.asp#ixzz1q2NczAIu.)

Lean

Also referred to as lean manufacturing, lean enterprise, or lean production. "The core idea is to maximize customer value while minimizing waste. Simply, lean means creating more value for customers with fewer resources." The definitions and usage of "lean" vary depending on context and application. The origin of the word in business can be linked back to the 90s. ("What is Lean?" Lean Enterprise Institute, http://www.lean.org/whatslean/.)

"Lean manufacturing is a management philosophy derived mostly from the Toyota Production System (TPS)." The key focus is around the reduction of waste whiling focusing on delivering value to the customer.
("Lean manufacturing," *Wikipedia*,
https://en.wikipedia.org/wiki/Lean_manufacturing.)

Lean Startup

"Lean startup is a term coined and trade marked by Eric Ries. His method advocates the creation of rapid prototypes designed to test market assumptions, and uses customer feedback to evolve them much faster than via more traditional product development practices, such as the Waterfall model. It is not uncommon to see Lean Startups release new code to production multiple times a day, often using a practice known as Continuous Deployment." You should note the slight differences between lean and bootstrapping.
("Lean startup," *Wikipedia*,
https://en.wikipedia.org/wiki/Lean_startup.)
"Bootstrapping provides a strategic roadmap for achieving sustainability through customer funding (i.e., charging customers), lean startups provide a more tactical approach to achieving those goals through validated learning." Note that a bootstrap

and lean startup have differences and bootstrapping does not mean spending any money.

AN EXAMPLE OF 3 STAGES OF A LEAN STARTUP:

1. Customer Discover (Problem/Solution Fit)
2. Customer Validation (Product/Market Fit)
3. Customer Creation (Scale)

("Bootstrapping a lean startup," Ash Maurya, https://leanstack.com/bootstrapping-a-lean-startup/, http://www.ashmaurya.com/2010/03/bootstrapping-a-lean-startup/ [site discontinued].)

Lean Startup Loop

The lean startup loop is the steering wheel of Build-Measure-Learn, a process that tells if and when to make a sharp turn (known as a pivot) and shift direction with agility (known as an iteration) altering plans inch by inch. The process creates disruptive innovation on a continuous basis through experiment, steer, leap, measure, pivot, or preserve.

Nondisclosure Agreement (NDA)

"A nondisclosure agreement (NDA), also known as a confidentiality agreement, is a legal contract between you and another party not to disclose information that you have shared for a specific purpose." Such agreements are used to discourage employees and/or business contracts from releasing sensitive information to others. It is important that you consult with a legal adviser about the content scope of such a document. ("Intellectual property and your work," gov.uk, https://www.gov.uk/intellectual-property-an-overview.)

Persona

Creating buyer personas is the process of conducting one-on-one interviews with customers to get a handle on their mind-sets, understand their purchasing decisions, and build three-dimensional profiles of real buyers. Buyer personas are examples or archetypes of real buyers that allow marketers to craft strategies to promote products and services to the people who might buy them.

Pivot

"It means to change direction. More specifically, to make a structured course correction with a business idea, and then to test a new hypothesis or new business model to see if it works better." Companies usually pivot when their current idea is not working or has lost momentum. However, you may pivot when you have launched an early version of your product/idea (prototype) and it needs improvement.

("Proceed or pivot?" Beat the GMAT, February 27, 2012, http://www.beatthegmat.com/mba/2012/02/27/proceed-or-pivot.)

Eric Ries suggests "designing products with the smallest set of features to please a customer base, and moving products into the marketplace quickly to test reaction, then iterating." (Martin Zwilling, "Top 10 Ways Entrepreneurs Pivot a Lean Startup," *Forbes*, September 16, 2011, www.forbes.com/sites/martinzwilling/2011/09/16/top-10-ways-entrepreneurs-pivot-a-lean-startup/.)

Product/market fit

When your product matches what customers in a specific market are interested in buying. (*Disciplined Entrepreneurship*, Bill Aulet, [New Jersey: Wiley & Sons, 2013], 263.)

Target customer

A group of customers in a market that you intend to sell the same product to. They share many characteristics and would all reasonably buy a particular product. (*Disciplined Entrepreneurship*, Bill Aulet, [New Jersey: Wiley & Sons, 2013].)

Total addressable market (TAM)

The amount of annual revenue your business would earn if you achieved 100 percent market share in a market. Expressed in terms of dollars per year. (*Disciplined Entrepreneurship*, Bill Aulet, [New Jersey: Wiley & Sons, 2013].)

USP, Unique Selling Proposition

The factor or consideration presented by a seller as the reason that one product or service is different from and better than that of a competitor. Using a USP in promotion and sales activities highlights your unique benefits and improves its effectiveness. It means delivering value and results to your customers. The USP answers four questions: Who is your target audience? What is the problem to be solved? What are list of the biggest distinctive benefits? What is the definition of your promise? These facts are then combined, reworked, and cut down.

Venture Capital (VC)

"Venture capital provides long-term, committed share capital to help unquoted companies grow and succeed. Obtaining venture capital is very different from raising a loan. Lenders have a legal right to interest on a loan and repayment of the capital, irrespective of your success or failure. Venture capital is invested in exchange for a stake in your company and, as shareholders, the investors' returns are dependent upon the growth and profitability of your business." There are differing views on taking funding from Venture Capital investors. Some argue that the involvement of VC in early startups reduces the "entrepreneurial" spirit and changes the direction of the company due to the overhanging financial commitment.

"Venture capital firms are only interested in companies with high growth prospects that are managed by experienced and ambitious teams who are capable of turning their business plan into a reality."

("Is venture capital for you?" Startups, accessed October 3, 2015, http://startups.co.uk/is-venture-capital-for-you/.)

The purpose of this evidence-based entrepreneurship (a.k.a. lean or smart startup) anthology is to help consolidate divergent works to help everyone better understand its meaning. This compendium can serve as a basis for further research. Every effort has been made to ascribe sources to their author or creator.

RESOURCES

For Experts –
Steve Blank, @sgblank, http://steveblank.com
Eric Ries, @ericries, http://theleanstartup.com
Bill Aulet, @BillAulet, http://entrepreneurship.mit.edu/

For Agile Development –
Trello, https://trello.com
Lean Kit, http://leankit.com

For Current Entrepreneurship Information –
http://clintoneday.com/category/current/

For Research –
Survey Monkey, http://surveymonkey.com
Validately, https://validately.com

For Testing –
KISS Metrics, http://www.kissmetrics.com
Google, http://google.com/analytics

And Others –
SBA Office of Advocacy, https://www.sba.gov
US Census Bureau, http://www.census.gov
Office of Disability Employment Policy, http://www.dol.gov/odep/
Epicenter, http://epicenter.stanford.edu/

Lean Startup Podcast, https://www.voiceamerica.com/episode/94653/understanding-lean-startup-evidenced-based-entrepreneurship

BIBLIOGRAPHY

Blank, Steven. "Why the lean start-up changes everything." *Harvard Business Review*, May 2013.

"Case Studies." The Lean Startup. Accessed June 4, 2015. http://theleanstartup.com/casestudies.

Cooper, Brant and Patrick Vlaskovits. *The Entrepreneur's Guide to Customer Development: A Cheat Sheet to the Four Steps of the Epiphany* (Cooper-Vlaskovits, 2010).

FDA Voice. "Making a Difference: Innovation Pathway and Entrepreneurs in Residence." US Department of Health and Human Services. April 10, 2012. http://blogs.fda.gov/fdavoice/index.php/2012/04/making-a-difference-innovation-pathway-and-entrepreneurs-in-residence/.

Harvard Business School. "Teaching a 'Lean Startup' Strategy." Working Knowledge. Published April 11, 2011. http://hbswk.hbs.edu/item/6659.html.

Lester Center for Entrepreneurship. "NSF Innovation Corps." http://lester.entrepreneurship.berkeley.edu/programs/nsf-innovation-corps/.

Maurya, Ash. "Why Lean Canvas vs. Business Model Canvas?" Lean Stack. Published February 27, 2012. https://leanstack.com/why-lean-canvas/.

UniTel Voice. *The Bootstrapper's Survival Pack* (UniTel Voice, 2015). http://startup.unitelvoice.com/wp-content/uploads/2015/12/Startup-Stockpile-Bootstrappers-Survival-Pack.pdf.

Rokop, Nik. "IPRO 397 Business Model Canvas." Presented at Spring 2015 IPRO Day, hosted by the Illinois Institute of Technology Stuart School of Business on April 24, 2015.

Roth, Carol. *The Entrepreneur Equation: Evaluating the Realities, Risks, and Rewards of Having Your Own Business* (Dallas: BenBella Books, 2011).

"Small Business Facts." SBA Office of Advocacy. Published March 2012. http://theleanstartup.com/casestudies.

"The Startup Dictionary – Learning the Lingo #2." Spark n Launch: Biz Startup Tech Blog. Published March 24, 2012. https://sparknlaunch.wordpress.com/2012/03/24/the-startup-dictionary-learning-the-lingo-2/.

"The Ultimate Glossary of Learn for Social Good." Lean Impact. Published October 2013. http://www.leanimpact.org/wp-content/uploads/2013/10/The-Ultimate-Glossary-of-Lean-for-Social-Good-Lean-Impact.pdf.

ABOUT THE AUTHOR

Clint Day serves as Entrepreneur in Residence at State College of Florida. He was a serial entrepreneur who founded three insurance entities in Florida and Georgia. Professionally qualified by the AACSB business school association, Clint holds an MBA in entrepreneurship. He has been certified by the Babson SEE, Kauffman Ice House, UF Experiential Classroom, Lean LaunchPad, and Network for Teaching Entrepreneurship courses. He wrote the first entrepreneurship quick study guide for Bar Charts, Inc. as well the how-to entrepreneurship book *Set Your Own Salary* published by BookLogix. He trains Florida veterans and active military in entrepreneurship under a state grant using lean startup.

Clinton E. Day, MBA
http://clintoneday.com (See heading "Specialties" on website)